The Complete Coach

Integrating Well-Being and Success in Athletic Programs

Eddie J Hamilton, M.Ed

Copyright © 2024 Eddie J Hamilton, M.Ed

All rights reserved. No part of this book may be reproduced or used in any manner without the prior written permission of the copyright owner, except for the use of brief quotations in a book review.

PAPERBACK ISBN:

979-8-9889111-2-8

To request permissions, contact the author at:

ejhamilton@eddiejhamilton.com

Published & Printed by

Beyond 94 Feet Publishing Co.

Houston, Tx

Table of Contents

Setting the Foundation for Your Program vii
Chapter 1: Laying the Groundwork 1
Chapter 2: Vision and Mission 7
Chapter 3: Defining Success 14
Chapter 4: Core Values and Principles 20
Chapter 5: Early Steps and Strategic Goals 26
Chapter 6: Building a Coaching Philosophy 32
Chapter 7: Sustainable Philosophies 39
Chapter 8: Core Values and Mission Integration 46
Chapter 9: Integration of Well-being 58
Chapter 10: The Importance of Coach Well-being 65
Chapter 11: Recognizing the Signs of Stress and Burnout 71
Chapter 12: Practical Self-Care Strategies 77
Chapter 13: Building a Supportive Network 83
Chapter 14: Integrating Self-Care into Daily Routines 89

Welcome, Coach!

Imagine a coaching environment where success isn't just measured by wins or losses, but also by the well-being and personal growth of both the coach and their athletes. This is the vision of "The Complete Coach: Integrating Well-Being and Success in Athletic Programs," a book that goes beyond traditional coaching techniques to emphasize the importance of a coach's health and happiness in fostering a successful program.

Drawing from years of experience as an educator and basketball coach, coupled with deep-rooted faith and personal challenges, I, crafted a philosophy that integrates well-being with the art of coaching. This book is born from a journey that began with personal turmoil—facing conflicts between personal desires and professional integrity, which nearly jeopardized my family and career. At a critical juncture, I embraced a transformative path, inviting spirituality to guide my actions, aligning my personal and professional life with my core values.

This transformation was more than just personal improvement; it substantially boosted my coaching effectiveness. My basketball program rose to become one of the top in the state, showcasing the deep link between a coach's well-being and their professional success. This experience highlighted the potential to make a significant difference in the lives of both coaches and athletes, ultimately leading to the creation of "The Coaches Code."

In this book, I share insights and practical strategies to help you, the coach, navigate the complexities of the coaching world while maintaining your well-being. You will discover how to set SMART goals, manage stress effectively, establish priorities, and balance commitments—each element aimed to nurture not only your professional success but also your personal health.

My aim is to redefine the essence of being a successful coach. By prioritizing well-being, we generate a ripple effect that elevates the entire athletic program, cultivating an environment where both coaches and athletes flourish in every facet of life.

Welcome to a new era of coaching—one where your well-being is as crucial as your playbook.

The Coaches C.O.D.E. Framework

C - Coach with Purpose
Clear Philosophy: Stick to your values and goals.
Strong Relationships: Build trust with players, coaches, and parents.
Continuous Growth: Keep learning and improving.

O - Optimize Team Dynamics
Effective Structure: Define clear roles and responsibilities.
Open Communication: Encourage honesty and trust.
Skill Development: Provide growth opportunities for everyone.

D - Drive Success Through Well-being
Holistic Success: Balance performance with well-being.
Well-being Priority: Focus on mental, emotional, and physical health.
Adaptability: Stay flexible to meet team needs.

E - Empower through Modeling
Lead by Example: Show the values you want to see.
Integrity: Always act with honesty and fairness.
Responsibility: Promote accountability in the team.
Self-Care: Take care of your own well-being.

Setting the Foundation for Your Program

Welcome to the foundational journey of building a strong, sustainable athletic program. As coaches, our mission extends beyond just crafting teams that win games; we are here to develop a program that thrives on well-defined visions and clear objectives, aligning with broader educational and well-being goals. The forthcoming chapters set the stage for understanding the essential early steps every coach must take to ensure not only the success but also the significance of their athletic program. Every great coaching journey begins with a vision. This isn't just about where you want your team to be at the end of the season; it's about understanding the long-term impact you aim to have on your athletes, the school, and the community. Crafting a vision involves deep reflection on what you value most and how those values translate into the athletic sphere.

1. **Define Your Core Values:** Start by identifying the core values that will guide your program. Whether it's integrity, perseverance, teamwork, or respect, these values form the bedrock of your coaching philosophy.
2. **Set Clear Objectives:** What are your goals for the team? While winning is often a measure of success, consider other objectives like player development, academic performance, and personal growth. These goals should reflect your core values and vision.
3. **Communicate Your Vision:** Once you have a clear vision, share it with your team, coaching staff, and all stakeholders. Effective communication ensures that everyone is aligned and moving towards the same goals.

Building a Mission Statement

Your mission statement is a clear, concise declaration of your program's purpose. It should reflect both your highest aspirations and the concrete goals you've set for your team.

1. **Reflect on Your Purpose:** Why do you coach? What impact do you hope to have on your players beyond the game?
2. **Incorporate Your Vision:** Ensure that your mission statement is a natural extension of your vision. It should not only guide your program's strategic decisions but also inspire your athletes and staff.
3. **Keep It Clear and Motivating:** A good mission statement is both inspiring and practical. It should motivate and guide everyone involved in the program.

Establishing Goals

Goals set the direction and benchmarks for your program. They should be specific, measurable, achievable, relevant, and time-bound (SMART).

1. **Set Long-term and Short-term Goals:** While your vision addresses long-term aspirations, your goals should bridge the gap between where your program is now and where you want it to be.
2. **Align Goals with Vision and Mission:** Ensure that each goal directly contributes to the overarching vision and mission of your program. This alignment helps maintain focus and prioritizes actions throughout the season.
3. **Involve Your Team in Goal Setting:** Including athletes in the goal-setting process can increase their commitment and motivation. It helps them understand their role in the program's success and develops their skills in setting and achieving goals.

Setting a strong foundation for your coaching program is essential for long-term success and the positive development of your athletes. This foundation stems from understanding your core values, establishing clear goals, and creating an environment of trust and respect. Prioritizing effective communication and continually seeking personal and professional growth ensures that you can lead by example and stay adaptable to the evolving needs of your team.

Remember, the strength of your foundation directly impacts the resilience and achievements of your program. As you move forward, always revisit and refine these fundamentals to keep your program robust and aligned with your vision. Your dedication to these principles will not only enhance your team's performance but also shape the future of each individual athlete under your guidance.

> "Any structure must have a strong foundation. The cornerstones anchor the foundation. For some reason the cornerstones that I chose to begin with I never changed." - John Wooden

CHAPTER 1:

LAYING THE GROUNDWORK

Welcome to the first step of your journey towards becoming a more effective coach. In this chapter, we will explore the foundational aspect of coaching that is often overlooked yet critically important: understanding your coaching identity. By the end of this chapter, you will be equipped with the "Program Builder Outline," a strategic tool designed to help you map out and clarify your vision, ensuring your coaching strategies are well-aligned and purpose-driven.

Understanding Your Coaching Identity

Your coaching identity forms the core of your approach and influences every decision you make on and off the field. It encompasses your values, your coaching philosophy, and your personal style of leadership.

When you are clear on your coaching identity, it becomes easier to make consistent and effective decisions under pressure. Whether you are addressing team conflicts, making strategic game-time choices, or guiding individual athletes through personal challenges, your core principles serve as a reliable compass. By deeply understanding and living out your coaching identity, you demonstrate authenticity and integrity, fostering a culture where athletes feel secure and motivated to perform at their best.

Furthermore, your coaching identity impacts how you build relationships with your athletes, fellow coaches, and the broader sports community. Strong, positive relationships are built on trust and respect, both of which are reinforced by a clear and consistent coaching identity. This allows you to inspire and influence effectively, encouraging growth and resilience among your athletes. As you refine and express your unique coaching identity, you not only shape a successful program but also leave a lasting legacy in the lives of those you coach.

1. **Identify Your Values:** Begin by reflecting on what values are most important to you in your role as a coach. Are integrity,

perseverance, teamwork, or compassion key components of your coaching style? Your values will guide your behavior and decisions, so it's crucial to define them clearly.
2. **Develop Your Philosophy:** Your coaching philosophy is an extension of your values and represents your beliefs about how your sport should be played and what role coaches should play. It affects how you communicate with your team, your approach to training, and how you handle competition.
3. **Personal Leadership Style:** Are you more of a motivator, a strategist, or a mentor? Understanding your inherent style will help you be more authentic and effective in your role.

The Program Builder Outline

The *"Program Builder Outline"* is a structured plan that helps you apply your coaching identity to the practical aspects of building and maintaining a successful athletic program.

1. **Vision Statement:** This part of the outline helps you articulate a clear and compelling vision for your program. What do you aspire to achieve, and how do you want your team to be perceived?
2. **Mission Statement:** Your mission statement should reflect your coaching philosophy and how you intend to achieve your vision. It outlines the purpose of your program and the principles that guide your daily operations.
3. **Goal Setting:** Set specific, measurable, achievable, relevant, and time-bound (SMART) goals that align with your vision and mission. These goals should not only focus on outcomes but also on the development processes that lead to those outcomes.

Chapter Summary

In this chapter, we have laid the groundwork for building a strong and sustainable athletic program by focusing on the core aspects of your coaching identity. By understanding and articulating your values, philosophy, and goals, you can ensure that your coaching methods and program structure are both effective and aligned with your overall objectives. Moving forward, you will be equipped to lead with clarity and purpose, enhancing both your team's performance and their overall experience.

> "It's the little details that are vital. Little things make big things happen." – John Wooden

Chapter 1 Reflection

"Great coaching starts with self-awareness and a clear vision. Your identity as a coach shapes every aspect of your program, ensuring lasting success on and off the court or field."

_____
_____
_____
_____
_____
_____
_____
_____
_____
_____
_____
_____
_____
_____
_____
_____
_____
_____
_____
_____
_____
_____

CHAPTER 2:

VISION AND MISSION

In this chapter, we delve deeper into the concepts of vision and mission—two critical elements that serve as the cornerstone for any successful coaching program. A well-defined vision acts as your north star, guiding every decision and action within your athletic department. Likewise, a robust mission statement ensures that daily operations align with your long-term objectives and resist the distractions of passing trends.

Setting a Clear and Actionable Vision

Your vision for your program is more than a lofty ideal; it's a precise and inspiring picture of what you aspire to achieve in the future. It sets the direction and defines what success looks like for everyone involved—from athletes and coaches to support staff and the wider community.

A compelling vision provides clarity and motivation. It acts as a beacon that guides your daily decisions and long-term strategies, ensuring that every action taken is aligned with the ultimate goal. When shared effectively, your vision can galvanize your team, creating a unified front where everyone understands their role in the journey towards success. This collective focus not only enhances performance but also fosters a sense of belonging and purpose among all members of the program.

Moreover, a well-articulated vision helps in navigating challenges and setbacks. When the inevitable obstacles arise, your vision serves as a reminder of the bigger picture, helping to maintain perspective and resilience. It instills a mindset of perseverance and continuous improvement, driving the program forward even in difficult times. By consistently reinforcing your vision, you build a culture that thrives on ambition, dedication, and mutual support, ultimately elevating the impact of your program on every individual it touches.

1. **Define What Success Looks Like:** Start by articulating your ultimate goal. Is it to cultivate top-tier athletes, to foster an environment of personal growth, or perhaps to win a specific championship? Your vision should reflect both your ambition and your values.
2. **Inspire and Motivate:** A strong vision does more than guide—it inspires. It should be compelling enough to motivate everyone involved to strive towards achieving it, even when challenges arise.
3. **Be Specific yet Flexible:** While your vision should be specific and clear, it must also allow for flexibility to adapt to changes in the sporting landscape or within your team's dynamics.

Guiding Decisions and Actions

With a clear vision in place, every decision made and action taken should propel the program towards this envisioned future. Here's how to ensure your vision remains central to your program's operations:

1. **Align Activities with Vision:** Regularly review activities and initiatives to ensure they directly contribute to achieving your vision. If something doesn't align, it might be time to reconsider its place in your program.
2. **Communicate Constantly:** Keep the vision in the forefront of everyone's minds. Regular communication about how current efforts are contributing to the vision can reinforce commitment and focus.
3. **Train and Empower Leaders:** Ensure that every leader within your program understands the vision and feels empowered to make decisions that align with it. This includes assistant coaches, captains, and even senior athletes.

Building a Mission Statement

Your mission statement is the "how" to your vision's "what." It should provide a clear pathway to achieving the vision and reflect the core values and culture of your program.

1. **Reflect Core Values:** Make sure your mission statement is deeply rooted in the values you identified as foundational to your coaching identity.
2. **Focus on Action:** Use action-oriented language to convey a sense of purpose and direction. It should clarify what you do, who you do it for, and the impact of these actions.
3. **Keep It Concise and Memorable:** A good mission statement is easy to remember and powerful enough to evoke engagement and motivation.

Chapter Summary

Having a clear vision and mission is crucial for guiding your athletic program towards its goals. These elements not only help in making strategic decisions but also in building a culture that aligns with your long-term objectives. By the end of this chapter, you should have a strong foundational understanding of how to effectively set, communicate, and implement your vision and mission, ensuring they serve as your program's guiding stars.

> "You have to have a consistent routine that prepared you to be great" - Jack Del Rio

Chapter 2 Reflection

"Your vision and mission are the compass that guide your program through both calm seas and stormy waters. Hold them close, for they will lead you to not just success, but fulfillment."

_____
_____
_____
_____
_____
_____
_____
_____
_____
_____
_____
_____
_____
_____
_____
_____
_____
_____
_____
_____
_____
_____
_____
_____
_____

CHAPTER 3:

DEFINING SUCCESS

Success in coaching cannot be confined solely to the scoreboard. In this chapter, we explore the multifaceted nature of success in sports coaching, broadening the definition to include player development, community impact, and personal fulfillment. Drawing upon the wisdom of renowned coaches, including insights from the legendary John Wooden, we will dissect various interpretations and models of success that transcend traditional metrics.

Broadening the Definition of Success

In sports, the immediate measure of success is often the win-loss record. However, as a coach committed to holistic development, it's crucial to consider broader dimensions:

1. **Player Development:** Success isn't just about developing better athletes but better people. Consider how your coaching impacts players' personal growth, sportsmanship, and life skills.
2. **Community Impact:** Evaluate how your program contributes to the community. This could be through community service initiatives, fostering a sense of pride among local supporters, or simply creating a safe and encouraging environment for young athletes.
3. **Personal Fulfillment:** Reflect on your own journey as a coach. Success also lies in your satisfaction and growth, the enjoyment you derive from coaching, and the fulfillment that comes with impacting lives.

John Wooden's Pyramid of Success

> John Wooden defines success as *"the peace of mind which is a direct result of self-satisfaction in knowing you did your best to become the best that you are capable of becoming."*

John Wooden, known for his success both on and off the court, provides a profound model of success that can be applied well beyond basketball:

- **Foundation of Hard Work and Enthusiasm:** Wooden's pyramid starts with the basics of hard work and enthusiasm. Success begins with a love for what you do and the dedication to do it well.
- **Building Blocks of Friendship, Loyalty, and Cooperation:** Success involves relationships. The bonds you build with your team, staff, and community play a crucial role in achieving collective goals.
- **Capstone of Competitive Greatness:** The peak of Wooden's pyramid is about being your best when your best is required. This means every practice, every game, and every interaction.

Chapter Summary

In this chapter, we've expanded the concept of success in coaching to encompass a wider range of impacts, aligning with deeper values and long-term goals. By adopting a more holistic view, you can foster a program that not only wins games but also contributes positively to the development of athletes and the community, ensuring personal fulfillment along the way. Use the insights from John Wooden and the provided tools to redefine what success means in your coaching career.

> "Success isn't measured by money or power or social rank. Success is measured by your discipline and inner peace" - Mike Ditka

Chapter 3 Reflection

"True success in coaching transcends the scoreboard; it lies in the growth of our players, the positive impact on our community, and the fulfillment we find in our journey. Embrace a holistic definition of success and create a legacy that extends beyond the game."

_____
_____
_____
_____
_____
_____
_____
_____
_____
_____
_____
_____
_____
_____
_____
_____
_____
_____
_____
_____
_____
_____

CHAPTER 4:

CORE VALUES AND PRINCIPLES

Introduction

Establishing core values is not just about setting ethical standards; it's about creating a culture that perpetuates success both on and off the field. In this chapter, we will delve into the essential values that should underpin every coaching program, including integrity, respect, perseverance, and teamwork. We will explore how these values shape player behavior, influence team dynamics, and contribute to a positive program atmosphere.

Establishing Core Values

Core values serve as the guiding principles for your program. They determine how team members interact, make decisions, and face challenges. First, involve your team in the process of defining core values. Engaging athletes, coaches, and other stakeholders in discussions about what principles are most important fosters a sense of ownership and ensures that the values resonate with everyone involved. This collaborative approach not only strengthens the commitment to these values but also enhances team cohesion and trust, as everyone feels heard and valued.

Once defined, it is crucial to integrate these core values into everyday activities. Consistently model and reinforce these principles in practices, meetings, and competitions. Use real-life examples and stories to bring the values to life, showcasing how they apply in different situations. Regular reflection and feedback sessions can help to remind and reinforce these values, ensuring they remain central to the team's culture and operations. Let's discuss how to define and implement these values effectively:

1. **Respect:** This value is about acknowledging the dignity of each player, coach, and competitor. Respect fosters a positive environment and promotes sportsmanship.
2. **Perseverance:** In sports, challenges are inevitable. Perseverance encourages athletes and staff to stay committed and strive towards their goals despite obstacles.

3. **Teamwork:** Essential for any team sport, this value emphasizes collaboration and cooperation. Teamwork ensures that personal goals never overshadow team objectives.

Integrating Values into Coaching Practices

Once values are defined, the next step is integrating them into everyday coaching practices and team interactions.

1. **Modeling Values:** As a coach, you are a role model. Demonstrating these values in your actions teaches athletes to embody them in their conduct.
2. **Value-Based Decision Making:** Use these core values as a framework for making decisions within the program. Whether it's dealing with discipline, choosing team leaders, or strategizing for games, let your values guide you.
3. **Creating Value-Centric Rituals:** Establish team rituals or traditions that reinforce your values. This could be a pre-game handshake to promote respect or a team huddle to emphasize unity.

Chapter Summary

This chapter emphasized the importance of core values in shaping a coaching program that not only wins games but also builds character and fosters a supportive, positive community. By carefully defining and consistently applying these values, you create a stable foundation for your athletes to develop not just as players but as individuals committed to excellence in all aspects of life. Moving forward, these principles will act as your compass, guiding every decision and interaction within your team.

"The values we put into action are joy, mindfulness, compassion, and competition" - Steve Kerr

Chapter 4 Reflection

"By embedding core values such as integrity, respect, perseverance, and teamwork into your coaching philosophy, you cultivate a resilient and unified team culture that extends beyond the field, fostering personal growth and lifelong success for your athletes."

_____
_____
_____
_____
_____
_____
_____
_____
_____
_____
_____
_____
_____
_____
_____
_____
_____
_____
_____
_____

CHAPTER 5:

EARLY STEPS AND STRATEGIC GOALS

The early stages of building or revitalizing an athletic program are critical. They set the tone and foundation for what comes next. In this chapter, we will provide a structured approach to help new coaches effectively navigate these initial steps. In this chapter we will focus on practical aspects such as assessing current resources, identifying key needs, and engaging key stakeholders—players, parents, and school administration.

Step-by-Step Guide to Starting Strong

Starting or rejuvenating an athletic program involves strategic planning and clear action steps. Begin with a thorough needs assessment to understand the current strengths and areas for improvement within your program. Collect feedback from athletes, coaches, and other stakeholders to gain a comprehensive perspective. This assessment will help you identify key priorities and set realistic goals that align with both the immediate needs and long-term vision of your program. Having a clear understanding of where you are starting from enables you to chart a more accurate and effective course forward. A well-structured action plan not only provides direction but also instills confidence and motivation among your team members as they see tangible progress toward revitalizing the program. Here's how to begin:

1. **Assess Current Resources**: Start by taking stock of what is already available to your program. This includes physical resources like facilities and equipment, as well as human resources such as assistant coaches and support staff. Understanding what you have at your disposal will help you identify what additional resources might be needed.
2. **Identify Key Needs:** Once you know what resources you have, the next step is to identify what you lack. Are there gaps in your coaching staff? Do you need better facilities or more modern equipment? Listing these needs will help you prioritize your actions.

3. **Set Immediate Goals:** Before you can set long-term strategic goals, you need to address immediate needs. This might include recruiting new staff, upgrading equipment, or organizing meetings with current team members and staff to understand their views and expectations.

Engaging Stakeholders

For an athletic program to be successful, it must have the support of its stakeholders. Here's how to engage them effectively:

1. **Players:** Start by holding a meeting with the players to introduce yourself and your vision for the program. Listen to their concerns and expectations. Building a strong relationship with your players is crucial.
2. **Parents:** Organize a parents' meeting early in the season. Communicate your goals for the program and how they can support their children and the program. Address any concerns they might have.
3. **School Administration:** Establish a good relationship with the school administration. Ensure they are aware of your plans and how they align with the school's objectives. Their support can be invaluable, particularly when it comes to accessing resources and facilities.

Chapter Summary

This chapter has highlighted the pivotal early steps and strategic objectives crucial for launching or reinvigorating an athletic program. By evaluating your resources, involving key stakeholders, and establishing clear, focused goals, you can create solid groundwork for future achievements. Keep in mind that the initial phase of coaching is equally about fostering relationships and gaining a deep understanding of your environment as it is about strategic planning and execution.

> "If you believe in what you're doing, you'll be successful. Just don't give up." - Bobby Bowden

Chapter 5 Reflection

"Success begins with a solid foundation built on assessing and addressing current needs, and it thrives through the active engagement of all stakeholders in the journey towards shared goals."

_____
_____
_____
_____
_____
_____
_____
_____
_____
_____
_____
_____
_____
_____
_____
_____
_____
_____
_____
_____
_____

CHAPTER 6:

BUILDING A COACHING PHILOSOPHY

A coaching philosophy is more than a statement—it is the essence of your identity as a coach and the blueprint of your program's success. This philosophy shapes every aspect of your team, from day-to-day operations to long-term goals, influencing the culture of the team and the behavior of its members. In this chapter, we will define what a coaching philosophy is, explore its significance, and discuss how to craft one that resonates with both you and your team.

Defining a Coaching Philosophy

A well-defined coaching philosophy not only brings clarity to your role as a coach but also establishes a foundation of trust and respect with your athletes. When athletes understand the principles and values that guide your actions and decisions, it fosters a transparent environment where expectations are clear, and mutual respect flourishes. This openness can lead to a more cohesive team atmosphere, as players are more likely to embrace the coach's vision and actively contribute to achieving shared goals.

Moreover, a robust coaching philosophy serves as a valuable tool during challenging times. Whether facing a losing streak, conflicts within the team, or external pressures, your philosophy acts as an anchor, helping you make decisions that align with your core values and long-term objectives. This consistency not only maintains your credibility as a leader but also reinforces the importance of resilience and integrity to your athletes, ultimately contributing to their growth both on and off the field.

1. **Core Elements of a Coaching Philosophy:**
    - **Values:** What you stand for as a coach.
    - **Objectives:** What you aim to achieve through your coaching.
    - **Style:** How you communicate and interact with your team.

- **Legacy:** The impact or mark you wish to leave on your athletes and program.
2. **Purpose and Importance:**
   - A well-articulated coaching philosophy ensures clarity and consistency in decision-making.
   - It helps in managing expectations and defining the path to achieving team goals.
   - It fosters a strong, cohesive team culture, enhancing motivation and commitment among team members.

Crafting Your Coaching Philosophy

Developing a personal coaching philosophy involves introspection and a clear understanding of your goals and values. Here's how to start crafting yours:

1. **Reflect on Your Personal Values:** Consider what principles are non-negotiable in your life and coaching. Honesty, hard work, resilience, and respect are common examples.
2. **Identify Your Coaching Objectives:** Define what you want to achieve through your coaching. Are you focused on winning, developing skills, or perhaps fostering a love for the game?
3. **Determine Your Coaching Style:** Think about how you prefer to communicate and lead. Are you authoritative, democratic, or a mix of various styles?
4. **Envision Your Legacy:** Reflect on what you want your athletes to take away from their time with you. Is it lifelong skills, memorable experiences, or championship titles?

Implementing Your Philosophy

Once you have defined your coaching philosophy, the next step is to implement it consistently across all aspects of your program.

1. **Communicate Clearly:** Share your philosophy with your coaching staff, athletes, and other stakeholders. Ensure it is understood and embraced by all.
2. **Align Practices with Philosophy:** Make sure that your training methods, team rules, and daily interactions reflect your coaching philosophy.
3. **Evaluate and Adapt:** Regularly assess the effectiveness of your philosophy in practice. Be open to making adjustments as your team evolves and new challenges arise.

Chapter Summary

Your coaching philosophy is the foundation upon which your program is built. It influences every decision, shapes the team's culture, and guides your athletes' development both on and off the field. By defining and implementing a clear and consistent coaching philosophy, you establish a framework for success that aligns with your values and objectives. This chapter has provided the tools and guidance needed to craft a coaching philosophy that not only directs your program towards its goals but also resonates deeply with all members of your team.

Moving forward, remember that a coaching philosophy is not static; it should evolve as you grow in your role and as your team changes. Continual reflection and adaptation will ensure that your coaching philosophy remains relevant and impactful, driving your program forward and fostering an environment where athletes can thrive in all aspects of their development. As you progress in your coaching career, revisiting and refining your philosophy will keep it vibrant and effective, ensuring it continues to meet the needs of your team and aligns with your evolving understanding of what makes a successful coaching practice.

> "My personal coaching philosophy, my mentality, has always been to make things as difficult as possible for players in practice, however bad we can make them, I make them" - Bill Belichick

Chapter 6 Reflection

"Your coaching philosophy is the compass that guides your journey, illuminating your path through every challenge and triumph. It is the essence of your identity and the legacy you leave with every player you mentor."

_____
_____
_____
_____
_____
_____
_____
_____
_____
_____
_____
_____
_____
_____
_____
_____
_____
_____
_____
_____
_____
_____

CHAPTER 7:

SUSTAINABLE PHILOSOPHIES

Sustainability in coaching goes beyond environmental concerns—it's about creating coaching philosophies that endure and adapt over time. This chapter discusses the critical importance of developing adaptable and resilient coaching philosophies that can withstand changes in team dynamics, school policies, and advancements in sports science. We will also explore how continuous education and self-reflection are essential for coaches to evolve their philosophies in response to new challenges and opportunities.

The Importance of Sustainability in Coaching Philosophies

A sustainable coaching philosophy is built on flexibility and adaptability, ensuring that it can withstand the test of time and varying circumstances. This means regularly reassessing and updating your beliefs and principles to reflect new insights, best practices, and the evolving needs of your athletes. By staying informed about advancements in the sport, changes in athlete behavior, and the latest coaching methodologies, you can continuously refine your approach to maintain its effectiveness and relevance.

Furthermore, fostering open communication and collaboration within your team can significantly enhance the sustainability of your coaching philosophy. Encouraging feedback and actively listening to your athletes' perspectives can provide valuable insights into how your coaching style impacts them. This inclusive approach not only helps you address any concerns or challenges promptly but also empowers your athletes, making them feel valued and integral to the team's success. By creating a dynamic, responsive coaching environment, you ensure that your philosophy remains a living, breathing framework, capable of adapting to both expected and unforeseen changes.

1. **Adaptability:** Your coaching philosophy must be flexible enough to adapt to changes without losing its core principles. This might mean adjusting your methods in response

to new scientific research in sports psychology or physiology, or modifying your approach to meet the changing needs of your athletes.
2. **Resilience:** It should also have the resilience to withstand setbacks, whether they are competitive failures, organizational changes, or personal challenges. A resilient philosophy helps you maintain focus and drive, ensuring the long-term development and success of your athletes.

Continuous Education and Self-Reflection

The landscape of sports coaching is constantly evolving. To keep your philosophy relevant and effective, you must engage in continuous learning and self-reflection.

1. **Ongoing Learning:** This includes formal education, such as attending coaching clinics, workshops, or pursuing higher education in sports science, as well as informal learning, like reading the latest research, learning from peers, or gathering feedback from your team.
2. **Self-Reflection:** Regularly reflect on your coaching practices and philosophy. Ask yourself what is working, what isn't, and why. Reflect on how your philosophy is perceived and implemented by your athletes and coaching staff.

Strategies for Evolving Your Coaching Philosophy

To ensure your coaching philosophy remains dynamic and effective, consider the following strategies:

1. **Regular Reviews:** Set a regular schedule (e.g., annually or biannually) to formally review your coaching philosophy. Consider the latest sports science developments, feedback from athletes and peers, and changes within your sporting environment.

2. **Incorporate New Insights:** Actively seek out new knowledge that can enhance your coaching effectiveness. This may involve adopting new training techniques, integrating technology into your coaching practices, or applying new psychological approaches to athlete development.
3. **Feedback Mechanisms:** Establish clear channels for receiving feedback from your athletes and coaching staff. This feedback is invaluable for understanding the impact of your coaching and identifying areas for improvement.

Chapter Summary

Sustainable coaching philosophies are not static; they evolve and adapt to remain relevant and effective. By embracing continuous education, engaging in self-reflection, and incorporating feedback, you can ensure your coaching philosophy stays robust in the face of changing dynamics. This not only enhances your ability to coach effectively but also ensures your athletes receive the most current and comprehensive guidance available.

> "Winning is not a sometime thing; it's an all-time thing. You don't win once in a while; you don't do things right once in a while; you do them right all the time. Winning is a habit" - Vince Lombardi

Chapter 7 Reflection

"In the ever-evolving landscape of sports, a sustainable coaching philosophy is your compass, guiding you through changes and challenges. Embrace adaptability and resilience, continuously learning and reflecting, to ensure your philosophy not only survives but thrives over time."

_____
_____
_____
_____
_____
_____
_____
_____
_____
_____
_____
_____
_____
_____
_____
_____
_____
_____
_____
_____
_____
_____

CHAPTER 8:

CORE VALUES AND MISSION INTEGRATION

When clearly defined and consistently upheld, core values serve as a compass that keeps everyone aligned with the overarching mission and vision of the program. Coaches and athletes alike can rely on these values to navigate daily decisions, both on and off the court or field. This shared understanding fosters a cohesive environment where individuals know what is expected of them and feel a deeper connection to the team's purpose. Core values such as integrity, discipline, and teamwork create a strong cultural fabric that supports the growth and success of the program.

Additionally, embedding core values into the fabric of your operations encourages accountability and promotes a positive, respectful atmosphere. As these values shape interactions and behaviors, they help in managing conflicts and guiding responses to adversity. For instance, a commitment to respect and communication can ease tensions and provide a structured approach to resolving disagreements. By continuously integrating core values into practices, meetings, and informal interactions, you build a resilient and unified team culture that can withstand challenges and celebrate achievements collectively.

Understanding the Interplay between Core Values and Coaching Philosophy

Core values are the bedrock upon which your coaching philosophy and program operations are built. They guide decision-making, influence program culture, and shape the behavior of everyone involved—from athletes to coaching staff.

1. **Identifying Core Values:** Begin by clearly identifying the values that are most important to your program. These might include integrity, which ensures fairness and honesty in all actions; respect, which fosters an environment of mutual esteem and acknowledgment; and teamwork, which emphasizes collaboration and collective success.

2. **Integrating Values with Philosophy:** Once identified, these values should be intricately linked with your coaching philosophy. This ensures that your philosophical approach to coaching is not just a set of ideals but a living, breathing part of daily practice.

Strategies for Effective Communication and Instillation of Values

The real challenge lies in effectively communicating these values and ensuring they are adopted and upheld by all program participants.

1. **Communication Strategies:**
    - **Consistent Messaging:** Use every opportunity, whether team meetings, training sessions, or official communications, to reinforce these values.
    - **Visual Reminders:** Employ posters, team gear, and digital media to keep these values visible in the team's environment.
2. **Instilling Values in Team Culture:**
    - **Modeling Behavior:** As a coach, your own behavior is a powerful tool for instilling values. Demonstrate these values in action, and you'll set a standard for athletes and staff.
    - **Reward and Recognition Programs:** Implement systems that recognize and reward behaviors that exemplify your core values. This could be through awards, acknowledgments, or privileges.
3. **Training and Development:**
    - **Educational Workshops:** Conduct workshops and training sessions that focus specifically on these core values, discussing their importance and practical applications.
    - **Scenario-Based Learning:** Use role-playing or scenario-based exercises to help athletes and staff practice responses that reflect program values.

Chapter Summary

Integrating core values with your coaching philosophy is not merely a strategic action but a necessary endeavor to ensure the long-term success and identity of your sports program. By effectively communicating these values and embedding them into the fabric of your team's culture, you foster an environment where athletes and staff thrive within a framework of shared beliefs and practices. As we move forward, remember that these values are dynamic; they require continual reinforcement and adaptation to remain relevant and impactful.

>
>
> "The kind of people who stop three steps short; I wouldn't call them losers, but they're never winners either. They always fall short" - Wayne Bennett

Chapter 8 Reflection

"Core values are the foundation of our integrity and the guiding principles for our actions. When embraced wholeheartedly, they not only define our mission but also illuminate our path to success, creating a unified and purpose-driven team."

_____
_____
_____
_____
_____
_____
_____
_____
_____
_____
_____
_____
_____
_____
_____
_____
_____
_____
_____
_____

Sustaining the Foundation for Your Program

As we conclude the first section of this book let's reflect on the key insights and strategies we've explored to lay a solid foundation for your athletic program. The journey of a coach is both rewarding and challenging, and starting with a robust groundwork is crucial for long-term success and sustainability.

Key Takeaways

1. **Understanding Coaching Identity:** We began by delving into the importance of understanding your coaching identity. This forms the core of your approach and influences every decision and action. By clearly defining your values, philosophy, and personal style, you set a tone that resonates throughout the entire program.
2. **Vision and Mission:** Establishing a clear and actionable vision, along with a concise mission statement, guides all operations and decisions within the athletic department. These elements ensure that your program remains focused on its long-term goals, avoiding distractions from transient trends.
3. **Defining Success:** Moving beyond traditional win-loss records to include player development, community impact, and personal fulfillment broadens the definition of success. This holistic approach not only enhances athletic performance but also fosters a positive and nurturing environment for all participants.
4. **Core Values and Principles:** Core values like integrity, respect, perseverance, and teamwork are essential for shaping player behavior and enhancing team dynamics. They create a culture that promotes growth and excellence both on and off the field.
5. **Early Steps and Strategic Goals:** The initial steps in building or revitalizing a program are critical. We discussed practical aspects such as assessing current resources,

identifying key needs, and engaging stakeholders. These actions ensure that your program has a strong start and is aligned with its strategic objectives.

By laying a solid foundation based on a deep understanding of identity, clear vision and mission, comprehensive definitions of success, strong core values, and well-planned early steps, you are setting your coaching program up for success that goes beyond the scoreboard. As we move forward in this book, we'll build on these foundations, exploring strategies to enhance team dynamics, develop coaching skills further, and foster overall well-being within your program.

Section One Reflection

"Building a solid foundation is not just the beginning of a journey but the bedrock of lasting success. As we move forward, remember that the principles of identity, vision, values, and early strategic steps are the pillars that will uphold your program through every challenge and triumph."

_____
_____
_____
_____
_____
_____
_____
_____
_____
_____
_____
_____
_____
_____
_____
_____
_____
_____
_____
_____
_____
_____

It's Halftime

As an athletic coach, I understand that my well-being directly impacts how effectively I can lead my team. It's not just about staying physically fit—although that's certainly important—but also about nurturing my mental and emotional health. I believe in the power of proper nutrition, regular exercise, and mindfulness practices to keep me at my best. And when things get tough, I don't hesitate to seek professional support. By maintaining my own wellness, I'm better equipped to support my athletes and help them reach their full potential.

In addition to personal wellness practices, I'm keen on creating an environment that promotes balance and well-being for everyone on my team. I've found that encouraging open communication and providing resources for mental health support makes a huge difference. It's all about fostering a positive atmosphere where athletes feel valued and understood. This holistic approach not only enhances performance but also cultivates a sense of camaraderie and trust within the team.

Coach, it's halftime! Before you dive into the dedicated chapters in this book that aim to enhance your wellness and well-being, I invite you to use the next four pages to define your wellness goals for this season and the direct actions you can take to accomplish those goals. This is your chance to take a moment for self-reflection to chart a clear path forward.

Take a deep breath and think about the aspects of wellness that resonate most with you. Is it physical fitness, mental clarity, emotional balance, or a combination of all three? Write down your specific goals and be as detailed as possible. Perhaps you want to improve your endurance, practice daily mindfulness, or establish a healthier work-life balance. Remember, the more concrete your goals, the easier it will be to measure your progress.

Once you've defined your goals, outline the specific actions you'll need to take to achieve them. This might include scheduling regular workouts, setting aside time for meditation or therapy, or planning nutritious meals. Consider any potential obstacles and think about how you can overcome them. By having a well-thought-out plan, you can stay focused and motivated throughout the season. I will see you in the next chapter, ready to continue this journey to optimal wellness together.

CHAPTER 9:

INTEGRATION OF WELL-BEING

In today's coaching landscape, integrating well-being into the athletics program's core philosophy is not just a benefit—it's a necessity. This chapter focuses on the strategic inclusion of mental, physical, and emotional well-being as fundamental aspects of your coaching practices. We'll explore detailed strategies to embed these elements into your program's daily routines and long-term goals, ensuring that well-being is not an afterthought but a key driver of your team's success.

Strategies for Embedding Well-being

Well-being encompasses more than physical health; it includes mental and emotional aspects that contribute to the overall health and performance of athletes. First, create an environment where mental health is openly discussed and prioritized. Encourage athletes to communicate their feelings and seek support when needed. Establish a system where regular check-ins with mental health professionals are standard practice, and provide resources such as mindfulness sessions, stress management workshops, and resilience training. By normalizing conversations around mental health, you foster a culture of openness and support.

Additionally, focus on building strong emotional connections within the team. Promote a supportive atmosphere where athletes feel valued and understood, and where their emotional well-being is acknowledged. Implement team-building activities that enhance social bonds and a sense of belonging. Teaching emotional intelligence skills, such as empathy and conflict resolution, can further empower athletes to manage their emotions effectively and maintain positive relationships, contributing to a healthier overall team dynamic. Here's how to integrate these elements effectively into your program:

1. **Mental Health Initiatives:**
   - **Education and Awareness:** Implement regular educational sessions to raise awareness about mental health issues such as stress, anxiety, and depression.

- **Access to Resources:** Ensure athletes have access to professional mental health resources, including counselors or sports psychologists.
2. **Physical Well-being:**
    - **Injury Prevention Programs:** Incorporate comprehensive injury prevention strategies into training routines, emphasizing the importance of proper warm-ups, cool-downs, and conditioning.
    - **Nutritional Support:** Provide guidance on nutrition that supports athletic performance and overall health, possibly including access to a dietician.
3. **Emotional Support Systems:**
    - **Build a Supportive Environment:** Foster a team culture that supports emotional well-being through open communication, trust, and mutual respect among team members.
    - **Encourage Peer Support:** Develop buddy systems or peer mentoring programs to create strong support networks within the team.

Practical Methods for Promoting Well-being

Integrating well-being into your coaching philosophy requires practical, everyday actions that make these principles tangible and effective.

1. **Daily Routines:**
    - **Mindfulness and Relaxation Techniques:** Start or end practices with mindfulness exercises or relaxation techniques to help athletes manage stress and focus.
    - **Regular Check-ins:** Have routine one-on-one check-ins with athletes to discuss not just their physical performance but their overall well-being.
2. **Long-term Goals:**
    - **Seasonal Well-being Plans:** Develop and implement seasonal plans that address the well-being needs identified at the start of the season.

- **Continuous Improvement:** Regularly review and adjust well-being strategies to respond to the evolving needs of athletes and the dynamics of the team.

Monitoring and Enhancing Well-being

To ensure the effectiveness of your well-being strategies, it's crucial to monitor progress and make data-driven enhancements.

1. **Use of Well-being Metrics:**
   - **Surveys and Feedback:** Regularly distribute well-being surveys to gather feedback from athletes on their mental, physical, and emotional health.
   - **Performance Metrics:** Track performance metrics that may indicate well-being issues, such as changes in performance, attendance rates, or injury frequency.
2. **Team Activities and Training Programs:**
   - **Team-Building Activities:** Organize activities that promote cohesion and emotional support, such as team retreats or community service projects.
   - **Tailored Training Programs:** Adapt training programs to include exercises that enhance not only physical but also psychological resilience.

Chapter Summary

Embedding well-being into the core of your athletics program is essential for the holistic development of athletes and the long-term success of your team. By establishing comprehensive strategies and practical methods for promoting mental, physical, and emotional health, and actively monitoring and enhancing these efforts, you create an environment where athletes can thrive in all aspects of their lives.

> "Always keep an open mind and a compassionate heart" - Phil Jackson

Chapter 9 Reflection

"Integrating well-being into the fabric of your coaching philosophy not only enhances team performance but also fosters a culture of holistic growth and resilience. By prioritizing mental, physical, and emotional health, we cultivate an environment where athletes thrive both on and off the court or field."

_____

_____

_____

_____

_____

_____

_____

_____

_____

_____

_____

_____

_____

_____

_____

_____

_____

_____

_____

_____

_____

CHAPTER 10:

THE IMPORTANCE OF COACH WELL-BEING

The well-being of a coach is instrumental in maintaining the overall health and success of a sports team. A well-maintained coach is equipped to handle the inevitable stresses and demands of the profession with greater ease and clarity. This resilience allows for more thoughtful decision-making and the ability to stay present and engaged, even during high-pressure situations. This chapter delves into why coach well-being is essential, not only for the individual's health but also for their effectiveness in leadership, decision-making, and the positive influence on their team. It also explores the consequences of neglecting self-care, which can lead to burnout, decreased team performance, and other negative outcomes.

Essentiality of Coach Well-Being

1. **Effectiveness and Decision-Making:**
   - A well-rested and mentally healthy coach is more capable of making quick, effective decisions during high-pressure situations.
   - Well-being directly impacts a coach's ability to prepare, plan, and execute training regimes that are both challenging and appropriate for the team's development.
2. **Influence on Team Health:**
   - Coaches often set the tone for the team's emotional and physical environment. A coach who prioritizes their health indirectly promotes a culture of well-being among the players.
   - The coach's attitude towards health and fitness can motivate athletes to adopt similar values, enhancing the overall health of the team.

Consequences of Neglecting Self-Care

1. **Burnout:**
   - Continuous stress without adequate relief can lead to burnout, which might manifest as fatigue, irritability,

depression, or a decline in health, affecting a coach's ability to effectively lead the team.
- Burnout not only decreases productivity but can also lead to long-term health problems and a decreased quality of life.

2. **Reduced Team Performance:**
   - A coach struggling with personal well-being may lack the energy and enthusiasm required to motivate the team, potentially leading to poorer performances in training and competitions.
   - The team's morale can be significantly impacted by a coach's diminishing engagement and presence, leading to decreased motivation and commitment among the players.

Chapter Summary

Coach well-being is not just a personal priority but a professional necessity that significantly influences team success and sustainability. This chapter underscores the importance of self-care among coaches, presenting a compelling case for why their health directly affects their team's performance. By integrating the strategies discussed, coaches can safeguard their well-being, thereby enhancing their effectiveness and prolonging their careers.

When coaches prioritize their own well-being, they become role models for their athletes, demonstrating the importance of a balanced lifestyle. This modeling sets a powerful example, encouraging athletes to adopt similar self-care practices, which can lead to improved performance and resilience in the face of challenges. A coach who practices self-care is more likely to inspire trust and respect from their team, creating a more cohesive and motivated group.

> "Rest and self-care are so important. When you take time to replenish your spirit it allows you to serve others from the overflow. You cannot serve from an empty vessel" - Eleanor Brownn

Chapter 10 Reflection

"Prioritizing your well-being as a coach is not just an act of self-care, but a commitment to the success and harmony of your team. By nurturing your own health and resilience, you set a powerful example, fostering an environment where everyone can thrive."

_____
_____
_____
_____
_____
_____
_____
_____
_____
_____
_____
_____
_____
_____
_____
_____
_____
_____
_____
_____
_____
_____

CHAPTER 11:

RECOGNIZING THE SIGNS OF STRESS AND BURNOUT

Introduction

Coaches dedicate immense energy and focus to their teams, often putting their players' needs before their own. This relentless dedication can sometimes lead to the neglect of personal well-being, culminating in overwhelming stress and burnout. This chapter aims to deliver essential insights on identifying the early warning signs of stress and burnout in coaches, highlighting the critical need for early intervention. By addressing these issues proactively, coaches can sustain their health and continue to lead with vigor and effectiveness.

Understanding the symptoms and consequences of burnout is vital for any coach striving for longevity and success in their career. We will explore practical strategies for managing stress and implementing self-care routines that not only enhance personal well-being but also positively impact team dynamics and performance. By embracing these practices, coaches can ensure they stay at the top of their game, benefiting both themselves and their athletes.

Identifying the Early Signs of Stress and Burnout

1. **Physical Signs:**
   - **Fatigue:** Feeling unusually tired or drained, even after adequate rest.
   - **Changes in Sleep Patterns:** Difficulty falling asleep, staying asleep, or experiencing restorative sleep.
   - **Headaches or Muscle Pain:** Frequent unexplained physical ailments.
2. **Emotional Signs:**
   - **Increased Irritability or Impatience:** Noticeable changes in mood, especially irritability with players, staff, or in personal relationships.
   - **Feeling Overwhelmed or Helpless:** Sensations of being swamped and unable to cope with daily responsibilities.

- **Reduced Motivation or Satisfaction:** Loss of enthusiasm for coaching or decreased satisfaction from achievements.
3. **Behavioral Signs:**
    - **Withdrawal:** Pulling away from social interactions, team activities, or **isolating oneself.**
    - **Neglect of Responsibilities:** Ignoring or delaying essential coaching duties or personal responsibilities.
    - **Increased Consumption of Alcohol or Other Substances:** Using substances as a coping mechanism for stress.

The Importance of Early Intervention

- **Preventing Escalation:** Early recognition and intervention can prevent stress and burnout from escalating to more severe health issues, such as chronic depression or anxiety disorders.
- **Maintaining Coaching Quality:** Addressing stress early helps maintain the quality of coaching and the well-being of the team.
- **Personal Health and Longevity in the Profession:** Proactive management of stress contributes to longer and healthier careers in coaching.

Strategies for Early Intervention

1. **Self-Monitoring:** Encourage coaches to regularly assess their physical, emotional, and behavioral health. Keeping a journal can help track changes over **time.**
2. **Seeking Professional Help:** Emphasize the benefits of consulting with mental health professionals when signs of stress or burnout begin to interfere with daily functioning.
3. **Establishing Support Systems:** Build a network of support that includes fellow coaches, family, and friends who can provide advice and emotional support.

Chapter Summary

Recognizing the early signs of stress and burnout is crucial for maintaining the health and effectiveness of coaches. This chapter has equipped coaches with the tools to identify warning signs and has emphasized the importance of proactive intervention. By taking timely steps to address stress and burnout, coaches can ensure they remain resilient and continue to perform their roles effectively, setting a positive example for their athletes and ensuring a healthier coaching environment.

Remember, the impact of sustained well-being extends beyond the individual coach to the entire team. When coaches prioritize their mental and emotional health, they create a supportive and thriving atmosphere that fosters athlete development and team success. This dedication to wellness cultivates a culture that values balance, making it easier for all members involved to recognize and manage stress effectively.

Ultimately, the health of a coaching staff is a cornerstone of a successful athletic program. Just as coaches invest in the physical and technical growth of their athletes, their investment in personal wellness is equally vital. This holistic approach not only prevents burnout but also enhances the overall performance and satisfaction within the team, paving the way for sustained achievements and fulfillment.

> "It's not the load that breaks you down, it's the way you carry it" - Lou Holtz

Chapter 11 Reflection

"Recognizing the early signs of stress and burnout is not just about preserving your career, but about nurturing your well-being to sustain your passion and effectiveness. By prioritizing self-care, you set the foundation for a healthier, more resilient coaching journey, benefiting both yourself and those you lead."

_____
_____
_____
_____
_____
_____
_____
_____
_____
_____
_____
_____
_____
_____
_____
_____
_____
_____
_____
_____

CHAPTER 12:

PRACTICAL SELF-CARE STRATEGIES

To sustain the demands of coaching and maintain effective leadership, it is essential for coaches to implement practical self-care strategies. This chapter provides actionable steps for self-care specifically tailored for coaches, covering physical, nutritional, restorative, and mental health practices. Additionally, it emphasizes the crucial role of setting personal boundaries to ensure a healthy balance between professional responsibilities and personal life.

In this chapter, you will discover actionable steps and insights on how to prioritize your well-being amidst the rigors of coaching. By embracing these self-care practices, coaches can enhance their resilience, foster healthier relationships with their athletes, and create a more positive and productive coaching environment.

Comprehensive Self-Care Strategies for Coaches

1. **Physical Activity:**
   - **Regular Exercise:** Engage in regular physical activities that not only keep the body fit but also relieve stress and improve mood. Activities could include yoga, running, or team sports.
   - **Routine:** Develop a consistent exercise routine that fits into the coaching schedule without adding additional stress.
2. **Balanced Nutrition:**
   - **Nutritious Diet:** Maintain a balanced diet rich in fruits, vegetables, lean proteins, and whole grains to support energy levels and overall health.
   - **Hydration:** Keep hydrated throughout the day, which is crucial for maintaining energy and cognitive function.
3. **Adequate Rest:**
   - **Quality Sleep:** Prioritize getting enough sleep, which is essential for recovery, mood regulation, and cognitive function. Aim for 7-9 hours per night.

- **Rest Days:** Incorporate regular rest days into the schedule to allow for physical and mental recovery.
4. **Mental Health Practices:**
    - **Mindfulness and Meditation:** Practice mindfulness or meditation to reduce stress, enhance focus, and improve emotional resilience.
    - **Stress Management Techniques:** Learn and apply stress management techniques such as deep breathing exercises, progressive muscle relaxation, or guided imagery.
5. **Setting Personal Boundaries:**
    - **Work-Life Balance:** Establish clear boundaries between work and personal life. This might involve setting specific times when work-related calls or emails are avoided to focus on personal time and relaxation.
    - **Delegation:** Learn to delegate responsibilities when appropriate to reduce workload and stress.

Chapter Summary

This chapter has provided practical and actionable self-care strategies tailored for coaches. By integrating these practices into their daily routines, coaches can maintain their health, enhance their professional effectiveness, and set a positive example for their athletes. Self-care is not just a personal responsibility but a professional necessity that enables coaches to lead by example and foster a culture of well-being within their teams.

> "Leaders who utilize self-care have increased well-being. A leader who prioritizes downtime, relaxation, and self-care discovers an increase in overall well-being and in multiple dimensions of performance" - Karina Mariama-Arthur

Chapter 12 Reflection

"By prioritizing self-care, coaches not only sustain their own well-being but also set a powerful example for their athletes, fostering a culture of holistic health and resilience both on and off the court or field."

_____
_____
_____
_____
_____
_____
_____
_____
_____
_____
_____
_____
_____
_____
_____
_____
_____
_____
_____

CHAPTER 13:

BUILDING A SUPPORTIVE NETWORK

Coaching, by nature, is a demanding profession that often involves managing the pressures of performance, training, and athlete welfare. For coaches to effectively handle these demands, having a supportive network is essential. This chapter explores the importance of such networks and provides practical tips on how coaches can build and maintain relationships that offer both personal and professional support.

Building a robust support network is not only beneficial for sharing expertise and insights, but it also offers a sense of community and belonging. When coaches connect with peers, mentors, and professionals, they gain valuable perspectives that can enhance their coaching strategies and personal growth. This chapter aims to empower coaches to actively seek and nurture these relationships, reinforcing the notion that collaboration and mutual support are key to long-term success and well-being in the coaching profession.

The Importance of a Supportive Network for Coaches

1. **Emotional and Psychological Support:**
   - **Stress Relief:** Sharing challenges with trusted individuals can significantly reduce stress and prevent feelings of isolation.
   - **Perspective and Guidance:** A network can provide alternative perspectives and advice, helping coaches navigate complex situations with greater clarity.
2. **Professional Development:**
   - **Skill Enhancement:** Interaction with peers and mentors can facilitate the continuous improvement of coaching skills and strategies.
   - **Opportunity Sharing:** A well-connected network can provide information about opportunities for advancement and professional development.

Strategies for Building a Supportive Network

1. **Identify Potential Network Members:**
   - Look within and beyond the immediate sports community to include peers, mentors, former coaches, family members, and professionals in related fields such as sports psychologists and nutritionists.
2. **Engage Regularly:**
   - **Consistent Communication:** Maintain regular contact through meetings, phone calls, or social media to keep relationships strong and supportive.
   - **Networking Events:** Attend workshops, seminars, and coaching clinics to meet new people and strengthen connections within the coaching community.
3. **Mutual Support:**
   - Offer support to others in your network. Reciprocal relationships are more robust and enduring.
   - Participate in or establish peer support groups where coaches can share experiences and strategies in a confidential setting.

Tips for Maintaining a Supportive Network

- **Be Proactive:** Don't wait for a crisis to reach out. Regular interaction can build a foundation of support that you can rely on when needed.
- **Respect Boundaries:** While building relationships, be mindful of personal and professional boundaries. Respectful interactions help maintain healthy, long-term connections.
- **Focus on Quality:** Rather than the size of the network, focus on the quality of relationships that genuinely contribute to your well-being and professional growth.

Chapter Summary

For coaches, building and maintaining a supportive network is not just beneficial—it's essential for managing the multifaceted demands of their profession. This chapter has highlighted the importance of such networks, providing practical strategies for coaches to establish and nurture relationships that support their personal and professional lives. By actively engaging with a diverse and dynamic network, coaches can ensure they have the support necessary to thrive in their careers and maintain their well-being.

> "If you want to go fast, go alone.
> If you want to go far, go with others." - African Proverb

Chapter 13 Reflection

"In the demanding world of coaching, a supportive network is not just a resource; it's a cornerstone of resilience and growth. By fostering connections with peers, mentors, and professionals, coaches not only enhance their strategies but also create a sense of belonging that fuels both personal and professional success."

CHAPTER 14:

INTEGRATING SELF-CARE INTO DAILY ROUTINES

Introduction

For coaches, finding time for self-care can be challenging due to the demanding nature of their roles. However, integrating self-care into daily routines is crucial for maintaining their health, well-being, and effectiveness. This chapter provides practical advice on how coaches can incorporate self-care practices into their daily lives, ensuring these habits are both manageable and effective. It also shares successful examples of daily and weekly self-care routines adopted by other coaches.

By prioritizing self-care, coaches can safeguard their mental and emotional health, consequently enhancing their ability to lead, motivate, and support their athletes effectively. Embracing self-care practices not only boosts personal resilience but also sets a positive example for the team, underscoring the importance of balance and well-being in achieving peak performance.

Practical Strategies for Integrating Self-Care

1. **Start Small:**
   - Begin with small, manageable self-care actions that can easily fit into your existing schedule without overwhelming you.
   - **Example:** Start your day with a five-minute meditation or end it with a ten-minute journaling session to reflect on the day's achievements and challenges.
2. **Schedule Self-Care:**
   - Treat self-care time with the same importance as any other coaching responsibility. Block out time on your calendar for self-care activities just as you would for training sessions or meetings.
   - **Example:** Schedule a weekly one-hour block where you engage in a preferred activity, such as a brisk walk, reading, or a hobby.

3. **Use Technology:**
   - Leverage apps and technology to remind you of self-care activities and track your habits. Many apps can help manage stress, promote better sleep, or encourage physical activity.
   - **Example:** Use a fitness tracker to remind you to move if you've been inactive for an hour or a meditation app to guide your daily sessions.

Examples of Effective Daily and Weekly Routines

- **Daily Routine:**
  - **Morning:** Start with light exercise like stretching or a walk.
  - **Midday:** Take short breaks during the day for deep breathing or a quick walk outdoors.
  - **Evening:** Allocate time to disconnect from work, spending time with family or on a hobby.
- **Weekly Routine:**
  - Select one day each week to focus on a longer period of relaxation, such as a massage, a hike, or engaging in a sport.
  - Dedicate an evening to planning the upcoming week, ensuring that your schedule includes time for these important self-care activities.

Chapter Summary

Integrating self-care into daily routines is essential for coaches to maintain their well-being and enhance their effectiveness. This chapter has provided actionable strategies and examples to help coaches establish and maintain self-care practices that are both practical and beneficial. By prioritizing these practices, coaches not only improve their own health but also set a positive example for their athletes, promoting a culture of well-being within their teams.

> "Managers and leaders are exposed to high levels of stress and pressure on a daily basis. By prioritizing self-care, they can build emotional resilience and reduce the risk of burnout" – Corporate Wellness Magazine

Chapter 14 Reflection

"In the demanding world of coaching, embracing self-care is not just an option, but a necessity. By integrating self-care into daily routines, coaches cultivate resilience, ensuring they can lead with strength, inspire with clarity, and nurture their own well-being alongside their athletes."

Section 15-Coaches' Self-Care: From Self to the Sideline

As we conclude the section on coaches' self-care, it's crucial to revisit the core message that has permeated throughout: taking care of oneself is not merely a luxury—it is an indispensable part of being an effective coach. We have explored various strategies and tools that can be integrated into daily routines, highlighted the benefits of prioritizing physical and mental health, and shared inspiring examples from other successful coaches. Embracing these practices is essential for maintaining your vitality and effectiveness as a leader.

Remember, a coach who invests in their own well-being sets a powerful example for their team, demonstrating the importance of balance and self-respect. By prioritizing self-care, you not only enhance your capacity to support and guide your athletes but also foster a healthier, more supportive team environment. The ripple effect of your well-being extends far beyond personal benefits, positively influencing the culture and success of your entire program.

Summary of Key Points

1. **Essentiality of Coach Well-Being:**
    - Well-being directly affects a coach's ability to lead effectively, make sound decisions, and maintain the energy and focus required for the demands of coaching.
    - The well-being of a coach sets the tone for the entire team, influencing team morale, performance, and overall health.
2. **Consequences of Neglecting Self-Care:**
    - Ignoring personal well-being can lead to burnout, decreased effectiveness, and health issues that not only affect the coach but also the performance and dynamics of the team.

3. **Practical Self-Care Strategies:**
   - Integrating simple self-care practices into daily routines, such as regular physical activity, adequate rest, balanced nutrition, and mental health practices like mindfulness or meditation, are crucial for sustaining long-term health and career longevity.
   - Setting personal boundaries and developing a supportive network are key strategies for maintaining a healthy work-life balance.

Reinforcement of Self-Care as a Necessity

- **Cultural Shift in Coaching:** Encourage a shift in the coaching culture where self-care is viewed as an integral part of professional development, not as a sign of weakness or an afterthought.
- **Leading by Example:** Coaches who prioritize their well-being are better equipped to inspire and lead their teams effectively. They serve as role models for their athletes, promoting a holistic approach to health and performance.
- **Sustainable Coaching Practices:** Establishing sustainable self-care practices helps ensure that coaches can continue to perform at their best over the long term, avoiding the pitfalls of burnout and other stress-related issues.

Conclusion Summary

This section has underscored the critical importance of self-care for coaches, providing them with practical strategies to maintain their health and effectiveness. By embracing these practices, coaches not only enhance their own well-being but also contribute to the success and health of their teams. As we move forward, let this understanding guide us in fostering environments where well-being is prioritized as much as performance.

> "My responsibility is leadership, and the minute I get negative, that is going to have an influence on my team" - Don Shula

Chapter 15 Reflection

"Prioritizing self-care is not an act of indulgence but a foundational necessity. A coach who nurtures their own well-being sets the benchmark for their team, embodying the balance and resilience they wish to instill in their athletes."

As we draw this book to a close, it's essential to reflect on the journey we've embarked upon together. The first part of our exploration focused on building a strong, sustainable coaching program. We delved into the importance of establishing a clear vision, defining core values, and implementing strategic plans that foster growth and resilience. By laying down these foundational elements, we've highlighted how a well-structured program sets the stage for success, creating an environment where both coaches and athletes can thrive.

Transitioning into the second part, we shifted our attention to the health and well-being of coaches, emphasizing self-care as a critical component of effective leadership. The demanding nature of coaching requires balancing numerous responsibilities, often at the expense of personal health. We've discussed practical strategies for integrating self-care into daily routines, underscoring the transformative impact of prioritizing mental and physical well-being. By embracing these self-care practices, coaches can sustain their energy, maintain their effectiveness, and serve as positive role models for their teams.

Building a successful athletic program and prioritizing self-care are not mutually exclusive endeavors. They are, in fact, deeply interconnected aspects of a coach's journey. By fostering a strong program and taking proactive steps towards personal well-being, coaches can create a harmonious balance that benefits everyone involved. As you move forward, remember that your dedication to both your program and your own health will lead to lasting, positive changes, empowering both you and your athletes to reach new heights. Thank you for your commitment to excellence and well-being and may your coaching journey be both fulfilling and inspiring.

The Coaches C.O.D.E. Framework

C - Coach with Purpose
Clear Philosophy: Stick to your values and goals.
Strong Relationships: Build trust with players, coaches, and parents.
Continuous Growth: Keep learning and improving.

O - Optimize Team Dynamics
Effective Structure: Define clear roles and responsibilities.
Open Communication: Encourage honesty and trust.
Skill Development: Provide growth opportunities for everyone.

D - Drive Success Through Well-being
Holistic Success: Balance performance with well-being.
Well-being Priority: Focus on mental, emotional, and physical health.
Adaptability: Stay flexible to meet team needs.

E - Empower through Modeling
Lead by Example: Show the values you want to see.
Integrity: Always act with honesty and fairness.
Responsibility: Promote accountability in the team.
Self-Care: Take care of your own well-being.

Made in United States
Cleveland, OH
13 November 2024

10593731R00067